Masterpiece

"Visionary of my

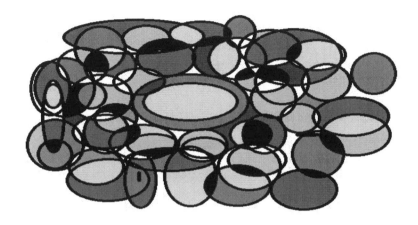

My Design

I was uniquely designed on purpose. There is nobody else on the planet like me.

1. What stands out about me?
   _____

2. What is the most different thing about me?
   _____

3. What do I like about myself?
   _____

4. What do I dislike about myself?
   _____

5. If I could change anything about the way I look, what would it be? I would make those changes because?
   _____
   _____
   _____

I was uniquely designed on purpose

My Purpose

1. I am very passionate about_____

2. My interests include:

3. My desires include:

4. I was created to become a/an_____

My Destiny

1. Define destiny?

2. Where do I see myself?

3. What steps must I take to get there?

Short Term Goals:

_____

_____

_____

_____

_____

_____

_____

_____

_____

Long Term Goals:

_____

_____

_____

_____

_____

_____

_____

_____

_____

_____

_____

_____

_____

_____

_____

_____

_____

_____

_____

_____

_____

_____

_____

_____

_____

I am on my way to my destiny. I will impact the nations.

Adjectives that describe me:

Compilation

Using information from each section, create a vision for your life.

My Life Vision

_____
_____
_____
_____
_____
_____
_____
_____
_____
_____
_____
_____
_____
_____
_____
_____
_____
_____
_____
_____
_____
_____

I Promise:

I will read my vision every day.

_____

_____

I will work on my goals every day.

_____

_____

I will see my vision manifest one day at a time.

_____

_____

Date_____ **Signature**_____

Notes